A Reality that is Not

A Reality that is Not

Edith Covensky

Translated from the Hebrew
by Susann and Ed Codish

HENSCHEL HAUS PUBLISHING
MILWAUKEE, WISCONSIN

Copyright © 2023 by Edith Covensky
All rights reserved.

Published by HenschelHAUS Publishing, Inc.
www.henschelHAUSbooks.com
Milwaukee, Wisconsin

Originally published in Hebrew
Translation by Susann and Ed Codish

Cover art: Rober Matta, *Etoile des Jardins*

ISBN: 978159598-947-5
E-ISBN: 978159598-957-4
LCCN: 2023936562

*To those whom I love
and to those who love me*

—Edith Covensky

Table of Contents

Foreword 1

A Reality That is Not 5
A Ballad 6
Evolution 7
I Sing to Myself in Silence 8
Fiction 9
A Debut Poem 10
Poetics 11
The Poem's Advantage 12
Music Rustles in Me 13
Madrigal 14
Murmurs 15
Invention 16
Tikkun 17
Simple Words 18
A Draft of the Night 19
A Sketch 20
I Remember all my Dreams 21
A Yellow Flower 22
Confession 23
White Night 24
A Parody 25
I Delude Myself 26
I Speak a Different Language 27

I Hold a Flower 28
Invention 2 29
Geometric Words 30
I Turn Everything into Words 31
My Hand is Stretched to the Sea 32
I Braid Night after Night 33
Waterfowl 34
I Cross the Night 35
I Invent My Love 36
For Proust 37
Archive 38
My Love Carries Me 39
Visions 40
The Night's Base 42
My Love Dictates All the Words 43
Pure Love 44
For Prometheus 45
I am Aware of Love 46

About the Author 47
Other Works by Edith Covensky 49

Foreword

Edith Covensky's current volume, *A Reality That is Not*, seems to me the most programmatic of her works. That is, these poems reveal better than previous collections the guiding poetics and philosophy forming her art. As the title itself reveals, her world exists on or in the ever-shifting borders between reality and non-reality. It affirms the value of both, even while recognizing that the mind is tugging towards reality and the imagination is resisting it. The clarity with which Covensky presents the struggle is unmatched in contemporary poetry. Once we understand the terms of *Agon*, namely, the conflict between the primary forces of reality pitted against fiction, poetry practically speaks for itself. "Day" is reality; "Night" is imagination, and Edith Covensky is, she asserts: "a poet of the night." Here is an example of how it works:

Fiction 2

>My memory is illusive
>Silent invention like the night
>Bound in such fantasy
>Larger than life
>Huge like my love
>Wandering among the bands of my dream.

> And then I select my poems from among
> all illusions
> Gigantic rising to the sky
> Circling under the geometry of stars
> Dissolved in gleaming color
> And the sequence of my tune.
>
> And then speech is required of me
> Flowing at the speed of becoming
> Creating a sun crowded onto the page
> Mixing in the order of my syllables
> Beating with the rhythm of music
> Active at such time.

The poem begins in a world of imagination. It gathers words to be connected to this world. They are memory, night, fantasy, love, and dreams larger than life. It is of ongoing interest in Covensky's poetry that love is most often associated with the imagination rather than reality.

The poem, *qua poem*, the poem as object is selected from the raw immateriality of her poetics, and her illusions. Yet, the poem needs a form, and for this there is the "geometry of stars" where the poetic encounters order. The poem's tune, too, needs a sequence in order to become real, to become at all, to achieve being independent of the imagination. The final stanza shows the poetic elements of imagination becoming actual speech.

Moreover, the poem's structural composites and sun become opposites of the night and dreams in the first stanza, and then the order of her syllables become the final poem. This process is necessary if we are to have a poem on a page. In fact, many of Covensky's poems are a struggle of imagination against order, reality and the everyday. We are left, however, with a poem in which imagination must survive.

There is another related conflict of images. God is important in this, and is often associated here with love, but not in an easy equation since love is human. Consider the following poem:

For Prometheus

> I wander among all times
> Circle across the shutters of the night
> Tremble in roaring wind growing stronger
>   in me
> Flowing with such rush
> Breaking on water.
>
> I steal my poem like Prometheus
> Rising in the sequence of my tune
> Under heavenly vaults
> Yellowing like a paper flower
> Adorning my longings.
>
>
> And then I paint with the color of the sea

Sing across circles of silence
Conceal my solid words
Measuring the sun
Crossing skies.

And then it's as if I touch God
Grow dizzy at the height
Stare with torn eyes
Abashed in a version of day
Edgy laden with such things
Flowing across the wrinkles of time.

Here, the poem is that fire Prometheus stole from the gods, but instead of descending with it for man, she ascends with it. The poet muses until she can, almost, "touch God."

In Covenky's poetics, it might be accurate to say that it's the *poetic* that pre-exits any other force of nature, allowing the poet to sing even amid the "circles of silence" often attributed to divine spheres.

—Ed Codish

A Reality That Is Not

My words quiver
resembling the night's lantern
and the web of silent stars
concealing my poem
explicit
naked spread out on the page
like a missive
like a deceit
playing among thousands of words.

And I continue to dream
living amid my desires
erupting
flooding my tune
with unlimited language
feeling its way in the dark
mumbling music.

And then I croon from yearning to
   yearning
wandering back and forth
marking the circles of wind
played with such rhythm
and speech whispering my love
singing in a reality that is not.

A Ballad

I bite off a slice of my love
splendidly skillful
wandering wild in amusement
radical boasting in the poem
clinging to such passion
stealing fire like Prometheus
with desire matching night.

And I am the dreamer circling on high
roaming above the sea's thunder
daring
staring at the sun
in a ballad resembling prose
flowing like Odyssean music
immense
tempting me in a huge moment.

And then memory is an open flower
living within me
truer than any words
feeling their way under the sky's rustle
mumbling my silence
active like the noise of stillness.

Evolution

I am childlike
loving the night
detecting stars
singing in such a language
with the noise of music
filling with words scaring me
playing an ancient sonnet
rustling things marked in the wind
melding with a funny voice like the sun.

And then I run to the sea
like a girl playing in sand
marking grain after grain
inscribing my verses on the scroll of water
dripping from bank to bank
leading to gloom.

My love is such that there is no greater
wandering in thought
anew time after time
clinging to stillness near me
like to the weight of silence
liquid with language bated in me
sizing my memories enfolded on the page
mixing in high fiction.

I Sing to Myself in Silence

I sing to myself in silence touching me
eluding the sun
curling in dim words
joining pain after pain
liquid in this chat
rising in me
collecting my memories.

The rain leaves marks on me
poured into the water's warehouse
as if tear pursues tear
flowing on the scroll
seeping into a yellowing photograph
full of sound
breaking among the wettest words.

And then I wallow in the sand
as if born from the ashes
stare at the stars blinking in the
    color of night
building my illusions bound in
    blue speech
almost novel
almost precise
painting for me the sky's height.

Fiction

My love stings my eyes
crowding into such fancy
elusive sad like the night
turning blue at a splendid moment
scattered across a drunken tear
building poem after poem whispering
    in me
quivering amid verses flowing at the peak
    of wind
folding onto the music's rhythm
melding on the scroll
wondering at such a tune
impressive occurring in me
as if I were the poet of water
as if I used the speech of rain
and the silence of collected yearning
sipping through time growing old
wrinkling on the floor.

A Debut Poem

I wander in my own realm
gobbling night
singing such a tune
dragging word after word
noting my love
free playing in me
washing over my dreams.

And I am
close to all revelations
arising from tipsy delusions
sketching my myriad longings
mixing among central words
as if from childhood
flowing at mid-sea.

And then the poem grows stronger
solid abashed playing in me
clear climbing to the sky
splitting stars echoing against one another
crowding above water
flowing in the spume of my words.

Poetics

I connect with each word in the poem
keep syllable after syllable
gather my memories under the
    whitest stars
as if gazing at me
as if rolling on the scroll.

And then I elude all times
circle high above
disband by the wealth of verse
crowding in me
bursting through my night.

How I wonder in the poem
in my sole illusive potential
like belief wallowing on the ground
wandering back and forth
mixed with the sun's circle.

How I sing against the choir of
    my longings
mixed in blue
flowing in time crossing time
and in such a splendid tune
climbing to the sky.

The Poem's Advantage

My poem is an advantage
solid like the foundation of the night
like belief
wailing from the dark
crowding under God among all the
    seraphs
with sound and trembling
scattering into the scroll of my poem.

And I am such a minstrel
living with great love
spread on the page
generous like the sun
curling in clear light
chasing heavens
melting into the blue.

Music Rustles in Me

Music rustles in me
echoing amid my many memories
in a discourse leading to the sea
bearing me from water to water
weaving my words time after time.

And then I mark my love
secretly playing
rustling with such laughter
resembling fiction making me a poem
adjacent to the thunder of the night.

And then the tune murmurs in me
whispers across the remnant of the flower
and the sun emptied on the page
burning syllable after syllable
silent gathering itself in clearest language.

Madrigal

I write poem after poem
in musical order
and confession gathering in me
whispering a flower folding in the
    rustle of the wind
spreading my dream in silence
    whispering in me.

And the rustle is pure like my love
abundant with my fragile words
    on the page
sliding syllable by syllable
curling in deceit
and desire blended with summer
hiding my yellowing verses.

My love never wilts
scattered on the page
wallowing in the rain
whispering this way and that
crossing my memory like the sound
    of the night
mumbling yearning after yearning.

Murmurs

My words crowd into the poem
rustling within me
flowing at the speed of the wind
unpacking memory after memory
elusive across the columns of the night.

And I sing with the greatest pleasure
melding between the hammocks
    of my verses
drumming with such music
in fragile musing
and a prayer echoing in song.

How love rustles in me
dissolving in the harvest of the words
sleepwalking in a summer's sonnet
and in time round as the sun
crossing stars inventing my rhymes.

How I am born anew
sailing on thin water
across the sadness of rain
and a moment in the making
with such high illusion and great love.

Invention

I invent my words as if from childhood
fragile wallowing on the page
murmuring longing after longing
with the greatest pleasure
insistent in the summer.

And then I complete all the sonnets
sing about the color of the night
in a version dissolving in the rain
    trickling through me
like a type of memory
collecting my devious melody
resembling the dark void.

And then I roll time into time
endlessly interpret my dreams
like love wandering in me
circling between verses
silent abashed
concluding my poem
trilling in the praise of the moment.

Tikkun

There is something in this poem:
like the fear of the dark
rolling among the puddles of words
crowded into the corridor of night
and love breaking in me
careful with the tune

And I repair my words
quick in the wind blasting from star to star
in a potential dream
trapping my love alive in the glory
    of the moment
like the flower of fantasy
and like a muse giving me tune after tune.

And then I talk to God
bound in the lofty discourse
twirling with the greatest temptation
fading in dissonant things
melding in a sun revealing fantasy
wandering in the thicket of light
becoming as if from childhood.

Simple Words

I live among the medleys of my love
amusing myself night after night
murmuring my fear
abashed in the flow of my memory
among shards of pain
grasping me.

And I sway from bank to bank
listening to the boom of the sea
roaring among the mounds of water
flowing with the rhythm of the moment
across the crimson sun
pulsing in lucid silence.

And then I am still like solid sadness
climbing to the sky
captive among all the stars
and between the folds of time
wallowing on the tracks of my poem
fading among simple words
hidden in the text
resembling a subtle illusion
whispering with minimal music.

A Draft of the Night

I am attentive to the poem
taking pleasure in the sonnet
    inventing my words
flowing on the draft of the night
across an old street
crossed in the version of the poem
useful like water music
and sad laughter.

And I write in my memory book
in black and white
and in the color of the sea
spilled on the page
bursting my syllables
joining into such a love
resembling the sun.

And then my poem is like God's work
revealed in holiness
in a utopia preserving me
suited to my speech breaking like clay
in fear bound in me.

A Sketch

My love trembles among the sheaves
    of the night
curling in great silence
collecting within me
hushing with measured words
as if hiding in the poem
as if holding onto stars
rising in yearning after yearning.

And I sing among the bars of silence
in a sketch coming from the sea
touching me
whispering my tune
wandering from bank to bank.

And then music ascends to heaven
echoing across the sun
caught in this fabric of light
coming into being
like a memory of love
spilled on time's diagonal.

I Remember All My Dreams

I hew word with word
as if from memory
gathering these things alongside those
with laughter trapped in me
echoing in the melody.

I remember all my dreams
wet from the rain
repeating my story in thought
    resembling night
flowing along the pier of time.

And then I sing among the seedbeds
    of my words
adorning myself with the sun crowding
    into this chronicle
wild in love touching me
dripping in the mumble of the moment.

A Yellow Flower

I write because of the dark
a night diver
crossing my musings
dictating my words in secret
rambling over the page
funny in wandering murk.

Memory is already gone
measuring my time like Bergson
rewriting words spilling into the sea
splashing among the seashells
playful in me.

I love music
trilling in a melody echoed in illusion
free in yearning rising in me
circling across the scarlet of the sun
blushing on the scroll
amid what's left of the yellow flower.

Confession

I feel protected in the poem
curled up in word after word
as if in fantastic music
bound in me
roaming from tune to tune.

The sun is a symbol
flowing across the tunnels of light
telling one star from another
trapped in dissonant longings
fading in time.

And I sketch my words in blue
as if drawing the sky
in an epilogue rising in me
across the field of God
bursting in my dream.

White Night

I grasp the strip of night
parallel to my tune
echoing in the color of the dark
across the sea's wrinkles
and memory swaying this way and that.

And I seed words with words
in language enclosed in me
and desire crooning at the edge
    of the street
like the howl of wind
mumbling in a different voice
giving birth to my love.

And then I gather longing after longing
filling with music made of words
like a medley of love bound with love
among things resembling rock and iron
wallowing like Sisyphus.

A Parody

I bear responsibility for every word I write
pretending to reach the truth
in a dream presenting my language
clear as if seeing the light
as if painting all the words.

And I draw my love to heaven's edge
almost childishly
crowding into such a memory
telling of night's sadness
from which I no longer have refuge.

And then my hand is outstretched
wild suiting me
moving to the center of the page
resembling a vestige of time
filling my poem.

I am lonely
naked trickling through thought
like yearning dripping water
flowing within me
resembling such delight
at work in a parody.

I Delude Myself

I delude myself
with matters of the night
crowding in me
like love curling in a dream
revealed to me
keeping still
flowing over my face
measuring my pain.

I am egocentric
feeling my way in the dark whispering
    on the page
like a wind circling above water
measured moving to and fro
leading to the sea
crinkling in this sketch.

And then I ask the meaning of words
mumbling my syllables sound by sound
intent on the music
resembling my love
adorning itself across the sun
funny in a sonnet drawn on the scroll.

I Speak a Different Language

I speak a different language
touching all the words climbing to the sky
in the darkness playing in me
among the remnants of stars
    inspiring light
across a web of things overlooking the sea
like naked memory
rushed on the page
bound in word after word.

And then I gather myself in the
    middle of the night
fold love into love
murmur in the rain
gliding on the page
across a wind burning my syllables
spread out this way and that.

And then speech is music
catching my illusions
wet trembling like water
moving from bank to bank
resembling my yellowing pain.

I Hold a Flower

I sense my love near me
whispering beyond everything I can see
in a drawing renewed time after time
pale
because of sadness
touching my words
braiding syllable to syllable.

And then I hold a flower
growing in the middle of the street
rising under the stars roaming from
    heaven to heaven
resembling such loneliness
tying longing to longing
wandering across the sea
singing with loudest voice.

Invention 2

My memory is elusive
silent fiction like the night
bound in such a fantasy
larger than life
huge like my love
wandering among the bands of my dream.

And then I select a poem from among
    all illusions
gigantic rising to the sky
circling under the geometry of stars
dissolved in gleaming color
and the sequence of my tune.

And then speech is required of me
flowing at the speed of becoming
creating a sun crowded into the page
mixing in the order of my syllables
beating with the rhythm of music
active at such a time.

Geometric Words

My words are geometric
lucid resembling the order of stars
glittering in a storyline playing in me
like longing in the middle of the night
curling in a type of fragile memory
growing old within me.

And I take cover because of the dark
huddling close to a great love
insistent breaking through in language
    marked on the page
like the color of the flower
fading in such a monograph
echoing in the margins.

My poem is ancient
(you say)
inventing my words in longing
among such things
like trees and the sun and the sea
crowded in me
playing day after day.

I Turn Everything into Words

I live in my expanse
sing ceaselessly
erasing the dark
flooding my poem's speech
bursting with love filled with flowers
fragile marking me.

I turn everything into words
trying hard with childish melody
echoing among seashells
clinging to obsessive love
speaking to me night after night.

And I wander in the wind
naked measuring my words
drawing a star round like the sun
blessing things I find in the street
silently stepping in solitude
surrounding me on all sides.

My Hand is Stretched to the Sea

My hand is stretched to the sea
touching water burbling in me
like my aging memory
elusive clinging to music
echoing in greatest solitude.

And I draw word after word
gathering my longings folded on the page
curling in the middle of the night
in a drunken sketch
whispering blue love.

How I feel the sadness
striding over hard ground
split between one yearning and another
trapping my words
wandering this way and that
rising sinking
climbing up to the heavens.

How I carry my love like the sun
and like a flower and a tree and sand
swaying on the scroll
wild across the bent of wind
clinging to this summer
with silk clad desire.

I Braid Night After Night

I braid one night into another
grow dizzy in thought quick like the wind
solitary among the fireflies of the dark
funny
leading my poem
wandering from bank to bank
flowing among the loops of water
bursting onto the page
murmuring in the thicket of speech
poured like memory erupting in me
naked in the trembling of the moment
gnawing at my sadness
Collecting my words
trapping my love
golden like the sun
moving in the middle of the street
curling among the bands of my longings
across the sadness wrinkling on my face
whispering my song
ancient sounding in me.

Waterfowl

My poem: a riddle
playing in me
curling under quickest stars
flowing at the height of heaven
in the order of words poured on the page
wandering among my musings
blending in the thicket of the street
leading to pain rolling this way and that.

My speech is occasional
drawn with blue pencil
bound in such a night
growing strong with laughter of a
    stubborn girl
circling on high.

I am free
resembling a waterfowl
flying from bank to bank
acting in fluid time
close to the sun
huddling at the edge of memory
storing my love.

I Cross the Night

I pass over the night
thrilled by the splendor
binding star to star
in a useful dialogue like the fabric of desire
strengthening under the sun
curling among quickest words.

My love is at the center of my being
invading the page
circling like a sea bird
with authentic language
doubling illusion with illusion
among bits of my memory
rising at such a time.

I am provocative
(you say)
singing in speech
echoing among my delusions
leaving behind fantasy after fantasy
rolling in a fragile text
spread out on the scroll.

I Invent My Love

I invent my love
ascending high
resembling the color of the sun
circling above the sea
in a possible dream
citing my words adorning me
wild growing as if from the ground.

And I erase night after night
chant in this monograph
laughing like a girl
mischievous tracking all the stars
growing stronger in the middle
    of the light.

I am funny
(you say)
walking on water
singing from memory
naked as if I have nothing to hold onto
careful in longing
kneeling in silence.

For Proust

I dredge up memories
braid day to day
like an enormous illusion
spectacular hallowed in me
exotic amidst all the magic.

My love lives in me
like testimony insistent on being
huddling at the moment of revelation
and the beauty of the night
and weakness trapped in me.

What is the sound of fear
across the arc of yearning
in a routine leaving in me all the dark
crossing my time
gliding on water.

What is the tremble of longing
and the murmur of rain
and the remnants of these thoughts
stubborn scattered among words
bundled in reverie after reverie.

What is love in the eyes
and the speed of light
and the tempo of summer
rolling among all the seashells
with ancient desire
roaring like the sea.

Archive

I archive my poem
solitary across the shards of the night
bound in the web of stars
locked in me
like naked love
building my illusions
in a most minimal story.

I discover the sun
and words with passing prose
like blue time
mixing syllable with syllable
revealed in play and parable
and in a cycle of things scattered
     on the page.

My writing is urban
(you say)
connecting dialogues
spinning in my funny eyes
wandering to and fro
swaying in loneliness pressed into me
enclosed in such a sketch.

My Love Carries Me

My love carries me
wild like the wind
rustling in the summer
adorned with flowers of my longings
and music born in me
sorrowful-funny.

I amuse myself
singing randomly
in such eternal prose
touching the simplest words
close to me
revealed in my basic speech.

And then I live from the poem's power
swaying from syllable to syllable
singing in sun-filled love
growing perfect in me
spectacular free
excited in a simple tune
playing on a most minor street.

Visions

I am solitary
sane in such a chronicle
hatching from the night
compressed into lofty thought
even in dreams
even in writing
growing on the scroll
amusing myself amid the abundance
    of words.

I live off the poem
and off the sun's flower
swing in the cradle of my page
mixing with such stars
hinting at my illusions.

My vision is ancient
filling with desire
free like the great sea
circling over me
curling among the rings of my words.

My speech is silk
born in me
on a rapid summer
crossing time
wet with rain
dripping like tears.

My poem is prophecy
braiding words together
rising with such clarity
like a love story
rustling in a hymn.

The Night's Base

My love clings to me
hesitant
fearing my fear
closing in on me
with pencil talk
binding star to star
with a great roar
sounding at such a time.

And I dismantle and build
watch the color of my dream
striding in the night
mumbling in such loneliness
whispering rain
across a bird rambling this way and that
wild singing at mid-day.

My Love Dictates All the Words

My love dictates all the words
rustling in the speech of night
like in a memory turning in me
speaking my mother tongue
in a huge poem
infinite.

And then I pile love on love
leading to the color of rain
and a girl's fear
drawing great love
swaying from pain to pain
howling in the hall of day
grasping me
biting at the darkest blue.

Pure Love

I sanctify my love
concealed among all words
rising to heaven
circling across stars
mixing in the canon of my poems
perhaps memory
perhaps forgetfulness
torn in a story.

And then it's as if I'm walking on water
singing aloud
insistent in song
rushed on such a street
twisting across the sea.

And then I walk on sand
rolling among the grains of love
pouring at the speed of rapid words
curling on the draft of my poem
breaking on the scroll.

For Prometheus

I wander among all times
circle across the shutters of night
tremble in roaring wind growing
     stronger in me
flowing with such rush
breaking on water.

I steal my poem like Prometheus
ascending in the sequence of my tune
under heavenly vaults
yellowing like a paper flower
adorning my longings.

And then I paint with the color of the sea
sing across circles of silence
conceal my words solid
measuring the sun
crossing skies.

And then it's as if I touch God
grow dizzy at the height
stare with torn eyes
abashed in a version of day
edgy laden with such things
flowing across the wrinkles of time.

I am Aware of Love

I am aware of my love
bearing desire after desire
mixed in such longings
playing in a song of sadness and joy
like in a dream growing stronger
rushing on the page
flowing across the sequence of time.

How I wander into the night
looking this way and that
silent collecting my words
close to longing
turning in a parody left on the scroll.

How I sing along
stepping across the sea
folding note into note
echoing in such a tune
breaking my illusions
marked by such silence.

About the Author

Edith Covensky was born in Romania, grew up in Israel, and has lived in Michigan since 1965. She has authored to date 35 books of poetry in mostly bi-lingual editions: Hebrew-English; Hebrew-French; Hebrew-Arabic-English, English-Romanian, Romanian, and Spanish. Among her titles are: *An Anatomy of Love* (1993); *Jerusalem Poems* (1996); *After Auschwitz* (1998); *Job was also a Paradox* (2010); *Matters of Sand* (2012); *Life as Fiction* (2017), *Portrait of a Poet* (2020), and *A Simple Woman* (2022).

Covensky is on the faculty of the Classical and Modern Languages, Literatures and Cultures Department at Wayne State University in Detroit, Michigan.

A book on Edith Covensky's poetry, entitled: *Under a Silky Sky: The Poetry of Edith Covensky,* written by noted Hebrew professor and literature critic, Yair Mazor, appeared in 2015. A second book by Professor Mazor entitled *Like a Coat of Many Colors—The Symbolist Poetry of Edith Covensky*, appeared in 2022 (both by HenschelHaus Publishing).

Other books by Edith Covensky

*Published by Eked and Gvanim Publishers,
Tel-Aviv, Israel, unless otherwise indicated.*

Other Words, 1985. (Hebrew)
Syncopations, 1987. (Hebrew)
Night Poems, 1992. (Hebrew-English)
An Anatomy of Love, 1992. (Hebrew-English)
Partial Autobiography, 1993. (Hebrew-English)
Origins, 1994. (Hebrew-English)
Synesis, 1995. (Hebrew-English)
Jerusalem Poems, 1996. (Hebrew-English)
Poetics, 1997. (Hebrew-English)
After Auschwitz, 1998. (Hebrew-English)
Metamorphosis and Other Poems, 1999. (Hebrew-English)
Steps, 2000. (Hebrew-English)
Electrifying Love, 2000. (English-Romanian)
Collage, 2002. (Hebrew-English)
Zohar, 2002. (Hebrew-English)
Anatomy of Love: Selected Poems 1992-2002, 2005. (Hebrew-English)
Variations on a Theme by Albert Camus, 2006. (Hebrew-English)
Black Rain, 2007. (Hebrew-English)
True Love, 2007. (Hebrew-English)
Testimony. 2008. (Hebrew-English)
Sea Breeze (Corona sonnets), 2008. (Hebrew-English)
In the Beginning, 2009. (Hebrew-English)
Pentagram: Selected Poems from 2006-2009, 2010. (Hebrew-English)
Also Job was a Paradox, 2010. (Hebrew-English)
Love Embraces Love, 2011. (Hebrew-Arabic-English)
On the Existence of Love, 2011. (Hebrew-English)
Allusion to Auschwitz, 2012. (Hebrew)
Matters of Sand, 2012. (Hebrew-English)
On the Border of Water, 2012. (Hebrew-English)
Microcosm: Selected Poems 1992-2012. 2014. (Hebrew)
Life as Fiction, 2017. (Hebrew-English)

Where to Go (Conversations for The Study of Hebrew/English), 2017, Rubin Mass Publishers, Jerusalem, 2017.
Portrait of a Poet. (Hebrew) Tel-Aviv: Beth Eked Book Publishers. Tel Aviv, 2020.
Portrait of a Poet. (English) HenschelHaus Publishing, Wisconsin, 2020.
Genesis. Buenos Aires (Argentina): Leviatan Publishing House, 2019.
Identities. Bucharest (Romania): Detectiv Literar Publishing House, 2019.
A Simple Woman.(Hebrew) Hulon: Oryon Publishing House. 2022:

CPSIA information can be obtained
at www.ICGtesting.com
Printed in the USA
JSHW022145130723
44540JS00002B/229

9 781595 989475